Imagine! 1

Oxford Read and Imagine

Ben's Big Swim

By Paul Shipton

Illustrated by Fabiano Fiorin

Activities by Hannah Fish

Contents

OXFORD
UNIVERSITY PRESS

2

Ben
Rosie's brother

Rosie
Ben's sister

Grandpa

Mom

Clunk
Grandpa's robot

Max
Ben's friend

Now let's read about Ben's Big Swim!

It's a sunny day.

'It's very hot,' says Max.

'Please can we go to the swimming pool, Mom?' says Ben.

'I'm sorry,' says Mom. 'I can't take you now. I'm going to the store.'

I can't take you now.

'I have an idea! Let's go to the beach!' Grandpa says. 'You can swim there.'

'Great! I love the beach!' says Rosie.

Grandpa shouts, 'Clunk! Where are you?'

'Here,' says Clunk.

Clunk! Where are you?

→ Go to page 20 for activities.

The children are sitting in the van.

'Take us to the beach, Clunk!' says Grandpa.

The children look at the houses and trees. Then …

'Wow! Look at the lights!' says Rosie.

Wow! Look at the lights!

'We're here!' says Grandpa.

The children jump out of the van.
Rosie is happy.

'Look at the sand!' she says. 'I want to
make a sandcastle!'

She takes a bucket from the van.

→ Go to page 21 for activities.

It is very windy at the beach today.

Ben looks at the sea. He is not happy.

'We can't swim here,' says Ben. 'The waves are too big!'

We can't swim here.

'I have a new idea!' says Grandpa.
'You can swim in a rockpool!'

'A rockpool? How can we swim in a little rockpool?' asks Max.

'We can use the van!' says Grandpa.
'Let's go, Ben and Max!'

You can swim in a rockpool!

Go to page 22 for activities.

Grandpa pushes a red button in the van and then …

'We're little!' shouts Max.

Grandpa drives the van to a rockpool.

SPLASH! They go under the water.

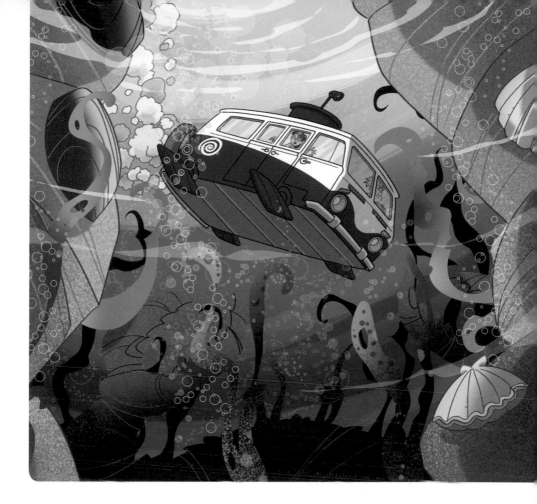

They see seaweed and shells in
the water.

'I can put the van next to that big shell,'
says Grandpa. 'Then you can swim.'

Ben points at the seaweed.

'What's that behind the seaweed?'
he asks.

→ Go to page 23 for activities.

It is a crab with big, strong claws.

'Let's go!' shouts Max.

But the van can't go. It is in the crab's claw!

Water is coming into the van now.

'Can you make the van big, Grandpa?' says Ben.

'No!' says Grandpa. 'The rockpool is too small!'

He runs to the door.

'Quick, Ben!' Grandpa says. 'Swim and find Rosie!'

Swim and find Rosie!

→ Go to page 24 for activities.

Ben jumps in the cold water.

He does not look at the big crab.

'Go, Ben, go!' shouts Max.

Ben is very scared. He swims and swims.

Go, Ben, go!

Ben climbs out of the rockpool.

'Rosie!' he shouts. 'Clunk!'

But Rosie and Clunk
are looking for shells.

They can't hear Ben.
He is too little.

He runs to the sandcastle.

Rosie! Clunk!

→ Go to page 25 for activities.

Ben climbs to the top of the sandcastle.

He jumps up and down and shouts, 'Here!'

'What's that?' says Rosie.

'It's your big brother,' says Clunk. 'But now he's little!'

Rosie runs to the rockpool.

'The van is little, too!' she says.

Rosie takes the van out of the water.

'Oh no! There's a crab on it!' she says.

→ Go to page 26 for activities.

Grandpa pushes the button. Now the van is big again!

Ben is big again, too.

'Where's that crab?' says Max.

'It's running home to the rockpool,' says Rosie.

'Let's go home, too!' says Grandpa.

They go home in the van.

Mom is taking the shopping bags into the house.

'We can go to the swimming pool now, Ben,' she says.

'No, thank you!' says Ben. 'No swimming for me!'

No swimming for me!

→ Go to page 27 for activities.

Activities for pages 4–5

1 Write the words.

store beach ~~hot~~ sunny

1 <u>hot</u>

2 _____

3 _____

4 _____

2 Write *yes* or *no*.

1 It's a sunny day.   <u>yes</u>

2 Ben wants to go to the store.   _____

3 Mom is going to the swimming pool. _____

4 Grandpa has an idea.   _____

5 They can swim at the beach.   _____

6 Rosie doesn't like the beach.   _____

7 Grandpa shouts, 'Ben! Where
   are you?'   _____

Talk **Do you like going to the swimming pool?
Talk to a friend.**

Activities for pages 6–7

1 Order the words.

1 van. / children / are / sitting / The / in / the

    <u>The children are sitting in the van.</u>

2 children / The / houses. / the / look at

    _____

3 van. / jump / They / out of / the

    _____

4 wants to / a sandcastle. / Rosie / make

    _____

2 Choose and write the correct words.

Grandpa and the [1] <u>children</u> are in the van.
Clunk takes Grandpa and the children to the
[2] _____ . Rosie is happy. Rosie wants
to make a [3] _____ . She takes a
[4] _____ from the van.

sandcastle   sand   ~~children~~   beach   bucket

Activities for pages 8–9

1 Write the words.

1 m i s w

swim

2 a v n

van

3 d i y w n

_____

4 e a s

_____

5 v s e a w

_____

6 c o k o l r o p

_____

2 Match.

1 It is	• not happy.
2 Ben is	• 'How can we swim in a little rockpool?'
3 Grandpa has	• 'You can swim in a rockpool!'
4 Grandpa says,	• windy at the beach.
5 Max says,	• a new idea.

Talk **Look at pages 8–9. How's the weather at the beach? Talk to a friend.**

1 Circle the correct words.

1 Grandpa (**pushes**) / **push** a button in the van.

2 Grandpa drives **to** / **too** a rockpool.

3 They go **at** / **under** the water.

4 They **seeing** / **see** shells in the water.

5 Grandpa puts the van next to a **big** / **little** shell.

6 Ben **points** / **point** at the seaweed.

2 Complete the sentences.

shouts   seaweed   ~~button~~   shell

1 Grandpa pushes a red __button__ in the van.

2 'We're little!' _____ Max.

3 They see _____ in the water.

4 'I can put the van next to that big _____,' says Grandpa.

Activities for pages 12–13

1 Choose and write the correct words.

Ben sees a crab. It has big, [1] _____
claws. The van is in the crab's [2] _____ !
Grandpa can't make the [3] _____ big.
The [4] _____ is too small. Grandpa says,
'Quick, Ben! Swim and find Rosie!'

crab   strong   claw   rockpool   van

2 Complete the sentences.

> **van** ~~**strong**~~ **find** **claw**

1 Ben sees a crab with big, __strong__ claws.
2 The van is in the crab's _____ .
3 Water is coming into the _____ .
4 'Swim and _____ Rosie!'

Talk Can Ben find Rosie? Tell a friend your ideas.

Activities for pages 14–15

1 Order the words.

1 doesn't / crab. / Ben / look at / the

_____

2 scared. / is / Ben / very

_____

3 rockpool. / out / climbs / of / Ben / the

_____

4 can't / Rosie / and Clunk / hear / Ben.

_____

5 runs / the / Ben / sandcastle. / to

_____

2 Look at the picture on page 14. Write *yes* or *no*.

1 The van is in the water. _____yes_____

2 The van is in a cat's claw. _____

3 There are three children in the van. _____

4 Ben is swimming. _____

Talk **Do Rosie and Clunk hear Ben? Tell a friend your ideas.**

1 Put a tick (✓) or a cross (✗) in the box.

 **1** This is a beach.

 2 This is a rockpool. ☐

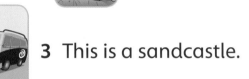 **3** This is a sandcastle. ☐

 **4** This is a claw. ☐

2 Write *yes* or *no*.

1 Ben runs to the top of the sandcastle. _____

2 Ben jumps up and down. _____

3 Ben is big. _____

4 Rosie runs to the rockpool. _____

5 Rosie puts the van in the water. _____

6 There is a crab on the van. _____

Activities for pages 18–19

1 Circle the correct words.

1 Ben **is** / **are** big again.

2 The crab is **run** / **running** to the rockpool.

3 **We** / **They** go home in the van.

4 Mom is taking the bags **next to** / **into** the house.

5 Now Mom can **take** / **takes** Ben to the swimming pool.

2 Look at the picture on page 19. Answer the questions.

1 How many children are there? _____three_____

2 How many robots are there? _____

3 What color is the van?

_____ and _____

4 Where is Clunk? next to _____

5 What color is Mom's hat?

_____ and _____

Talk Do you like this story? Talk to a friend.

Project

Story Characters

1 Write the characters' names.

Grandpa   Clunk   Mom   Rosie   Max   ~~Ben~~

Ben

Talk Talk to a friend about your favorite character.

2 Read.

This is Ben. He has a green shirt. He likes swimming. He doesn't like big waves. Rosie is his sister.

3 Write the answers about this story character.

Who is this?

What does she have?

What does she like?

Who is her brother?

4 Draw and write about a new story character.

Talk Talk to a friend about your character.

Picture Dictionary

beach

behind

bucket

button

claw

climb

crab

hot

idea

jump

light

next to

push

rockpool

sand

sandcastle

sea seaweed shell shopping bags

shout sit splash store

strong sunny swimming swimming pool

top van waves windy

Oxford Read and Imagine

Oxford Read and Imagine graded readers are at eight levels (Starter, Beginner, and Levels 1 to 6) for students from age 4 and older. They offer great stories to read and enjoy.

Activities provide Cambridge Young Learner Exams preparation. See Key below.

At Levels 1 to 6, every storybook reader links to an **Oxford Read and Discover** non-fiction reader, giving students a chance to find out more about the world around them, and an opportunity for Content and Language Integrated Learning (CLIL).

For more information about **Read and Imagine**, and for Teacher's Notes, go to www.oup.com/elt/teacher/readandimagine

KEY Activity supports Cambridge Young Learner Starters Exam preparation

 Oxford Read and Discover

Do you want to find out more about rockpools and the beach?
You can read this non-fiction book.

At the Beach

OXFORD
UNIVERSITY PRESS

Great Clarendon Street, Oxford, OX2 6DP, United Kingdom

Oxford University Press is a department of the University of Oxford. It furthers the University's objective of excellence in research, scholarship, and education by publishing worldwide. Oxford is a registered trade mark of Oxford University Press in the UK and in certain other countries

ISBN: 978 0 19 472267 4

Printed in China

This book is printed on paper from certified and well-managed sources

ACKNOWLEDGEMENTS

Main illustrations by: Fabiano Fiorin/ Milan Illustrations Agency.

Activity illustrations by: Dusan Pavlic/ Beehive Illustration; Alan Rowe; Mark Ruffle.